EL Education

There Is

More in Us

Than We

Know

A BOOK OF READINGS

©2018 by EL Education. All rights reserved.

EL Education

247 West 35th St., 8th Floor
New York, NY 10001
212-239-4455

Design by Mike Kelly

Special thanks to the students of Genesee Community
Charter School, Mapleton Expeditionary School of the Arts
(MESA), Palouse Prairie Charter School, Rocky Mountain
School of Expeditionary Learning, Santa Fe School for the
Arts & Sciences, and Venture Academy, whose art work is
featured throughout this book.

To view these and other examples of high-quality student
work, please visit modelsofexcellence.ELeducation.org.

CONTENTS

THE READINGS

There Is More In Us Than We Know

DEDICATION

There is more in us than we know. If we can be made to see it, perhaps, for the rest of our lives, we will be unwilling to settle for less.

Kurt Hahn

To those who help us see what is possible.

FOREWORD

To start a school is to proclaim what it means
to be a human being.

Tom James

Words are important; timeless words are precious
and fundamental. Words can clarify and unify.
They can touch things off and settle them down.
They can get at the heart of things and generate
insight and understanding.

Those of us who were involved, 25 years ago, in
putting together the organization and program
now called EL Education (EL) knew this, and
that is why one of our first tasks was to write
down a set of Design Principles (see pp. X-XI)
to guide and inspire our work. We were striving
for timeless words, timeless principles. We were
trying to update an existing text—Kurt Hahn's
Seven Laws of Salem, which he conceived for
his first school in Germany—that for punch and
directness was hard to improve upon. But it was
written in the 1930s and seemed dated in some
parts. And it was missing some other parts that
for us, in the 1990s, were important to include and
underline: "Diversity and Inclusion," for example,
and "The Responsibility for Learning." I like to
think of the 10 Design Principles as our original
set of readings.

Books of readings were part of the educational
tradition EL inherited from Kurt Hahn and
Outward Bound. Now we have created our own

There Is More In Us Than We Know

such book, including and retaining timeless and inspiring readings from the past and adding new ones from diverse voices to describe teaching and learning in the context of education today. It is noteworthy that readings that testify to powerful learning experiences have in the past come so seldom from classrooms and schools. We believe our work is changing that.

As an important step in that direction, this collection of readings comes from, in part, students, teachers, and leaders in public schools. They are authors of some of the readings and collectors and lovers of the rest. Like much of EL's best work, this book comes from the field.

Cyndi Gueswel and crew have done a great job of curating this collection. But this book looks to the future, and its most important part may be the blank pages at the end, where you are invited to add your own writings and favorite readings, both to help make this book your own and to help you contribute to the next edition. Aren't there timeless words, worth capturing and repeating, being uttered and shared in your lives and classrooms today? Might we all learn from them? If so, send them to publications@ELeducation.org so that we can continue to benefit from your collective wisdom.

Greg Farrell

Founding President and Board Member
EL Education
January, 2018 | New York, New York

PREFACE

As a young Outward Bound instructor in the 1980s,
I, like all Outward Bound instructors, used
readings as an essential part of every course. I had
my favorite readings for many different moments
on courses: the beginning stages when the group
was first bonding and adjusting to life in the wild;
the quiet, reflective pre-dawn time before leaving
camp for a peak climb; or the final stages, when
we were savoring every aspect of our adventure
together and readying for re-entry into the "real
world." I had other favorites, too: for the calm
moments in a river eddy before students pushed
off into the current to run a rapid, or before dinner
each evening to help us reflect on and illuminate
some facet of our day. The just right reading helped
to inspire us and, often, fostered deep reflection.

I didn't have a
book of readings
then—I compiled my
own handwritten
collection and added
to it continuously (see
photo). Some readings
I transcribed from
favorite book passages,
others I traded with
fellow instructors, and
some were passages I
took from my own expedition journals. Drawing
on the accumulated collections of instructors,
Outward Bound now has several great books of
readings. When I became principal of The Harbor

School in Boston, I reached for these books frequently. The collections never felt complete to me, however, in my new setting. So, once again, I began compiling additional readings that brought greater focus to the work of teachers and students within our urban school.

This book of readings is part of EL Education's 25th anniversary celebration. Scraps of paper tucked into notebooks, dog-eared pages from our favorite authors, and long memories have finally been brought together to create this collection. It reaches back into our heritage with Outward Bound and the Harvard Graduate School of Education to elevate the values that have guided us since our inception. And it draws on some of the seminal documents that have guided our work for many years—such as the Design Principles and the Dimensions of Student Achievement—that will carry us into the future. This book of readings draws on the accumulated collections of many EL Education staff, teachers, and school leaders and is curated with educators and students in mind.

I hope that this book will help you—in the ways that other books of readings have helped me over many years and in many roles—to inspire, reflect, and serve as a bridge between our unique personal experiences and the accumulated wisdom of our shared human experience.

Scott Hartl

President and CEO
EL Education
January, 2018 | New York, New York

INTRODUCTION

Much like taking a few deep breaths,
readings ground and center us. We use them to
spur personal reflection, and we share them to
build connections. Readings are multi-dimensional
gems of wisdom, colored by individual and
collective meaning-making about our humanity,
our beliefs, our values.

Readings are part of a long oral tradition, including
storytelling, debate, oratory, and philosophical
discourse. For EL Education, the roots of readings
go back to our history with Outward Bound
and founder Kurt Hahn, whose voice is well-
represented in this collection and whose words are
echoed in the title. With this collection, we seek
to honor our roots as well as amplify them with a
wide variety of diverse voices.

A well-chosen reading serves as a brief, yet
powerful offering that provides a group with a
touchstone, an inspiration, a provocation. Over
time, readings become like a series of tiny webs
that bind groups across time and space. Imagine
each reading as a fine thread catching dew and
light, stitching us together as we read them again
and again, with fresh eyes each time.

Each reading is also a doorway to a wider story.
When one strikes you, we encourage you to look
up the author or text and see where the path takes
you, to see what the greater context reveals. And
though the words you'll find here come from many
wise people, I believe we as readers are the true

authors, creating our own personal and collective meaning through our interactions with the text.

We hope this book becomes a treasure. We invite you to mark it up, make it your own, dog-ear pages of the readings that sing to you most. If you wish, jot dates and places in the margins when you discover or rediscover a reading on your own or with colleagues, students, friends, and loved ones—and personalize it further by adding your own gems in the blank pages at the end.

Wherever you are when the ideal moment strikes—whether on a solo adventure or seated in a circle during professional development or some other type of gathering—pull out this book to foster insight, wonder, delight, humor, and hope. Be reminded that indeed, "there is more in us than we know."

We hope this book will be carried in bags and backpacks, found lying open on desks, and held in the hands of crew members far and wide. May everyone's copy become shabby with love, like the Velveteen Rabbit. Let spying this book of readings be a sign that you have run across a fellow member of the EL Education tribe—a network of people who share a vision of teaching and learning that is meaningful, joyful, challenging, creative, and marked by contribution to a better world.

Cyndi Gueswel

Founder, Only to Grow - Coaching for Changemakers
Former Managing Director of Program
EL Education
January, 2018 | Loveland, Colorado

EL EDUCATION DESIGN PRINCIPLES

EL Education is built on ten design principles that reflect the educational values and beliefs of Kurt Hahn, founder of Outward Bound. These principles also reflect the design's connection to other related thinking about teaching, learning, and the culture of schools.

1. The Primacy of Self-Discovery

Learning happens best with emotion, challenge and the requisite support. People discover their abilities, values, passions, and responsibilities in situations that offer adventure and the unexpected. In EL Education schools, students undertake tasks that require perseverance, fitness, craftsmanship, imagination, self-discipline, and significant achievement. A teacher's primary task is to help students overcome their fears and discover they can do more than they think they can.

2. The Having of Wonderful Ideas

Teaching in EL Education schools fosters curiosity about the world by creating learning situations that provide something important to think about, time to experiment, and time to make sense of what is observed.

3. The Responsibility for Learning

Learning is both a personal process of discovery and a social activity. Everyone learns both individually and as part of a group. Every aspect of an EL Education school encourages both children and adults to become increasingly responsible for directing their own personal and collective learning.

4. Empathy and Caring

Learning is fostered best in communities where students' and teachers' ideas are respected and where there is mutual trust. Learning groups are small in EL Education schools, with a caring adult looking after the progress and acting as an advocate for each child. Older students mentor younger ones, and students feel physically and emotionally safe.

5. Success and Failure

All students need to be successful if they are to build the confidence and capacity to take risks and meet increasingly difficult challenges. But it is also important for students to learn from their failures, to persevere when things are hard, and to learn to turn disabilities into opportunities.

6. Collaboration and Competition

Individual development and group development are integrated so that the value of friendship, trust, and group action is clear. Students are encouraged to compete, not against each other, but with their own personal best and with rigorous standards of excellence.

7. Diversity and Inclusion

Both diversity and inclusion increase the richness of ideas, creative power, problem-solving ability, and respect for others. In EL Education schools, students investigate and value their different histories and talents as well as those of other communities and cultures. Schools and learning groups are heterogeneous.

8. The Natural World

A direct and respectful relationship with the natural world refreshes the human spirit and teaches the important ideas of recurring cycles and cause and effect. Students learn to become stewards of the earth and of future generations.

9. Solitude and Reflection

Students and teachers need time alone to explore their own thoughts, make their own connections, and create their own ideas. They also need to exchange their reflections with other students and with adults.

10. Service and Compassion

We are crew, not passengers. Students and teachers are strengthened by acts of consequential service to others, and one of an EL Education school's primary functions is to prepare students with the attitudes and skills to learn from and be of service.

There Is More In Us Than We Know

And don't worry about the bits you can't understand. Sit back and allow the words to wash around you, like music.

Roald Dahl

CHALLENGE

Plus est en vous ("More is in you")

Motto commonly used by Kurt Hahn at his schools

Success is to be measured not so much by the position that one has reached in life as by the obstacles which he has overcome while trying to succeed.

Booker T. Washington

Nothing ever goes away until it teaches us what we need to know.

Pema Chodron

We can let the circumstances of our lives harden us so that we become increasingly resentful and afraid, or we can let them soften us, and make us kinder. We always have the choice.

Dalai Lama

A journey of a thousand miles
begins with a single step.

Lao Tzu

And once the storm is over you won't remember how you made it through, how you managed to survive. You won't even be sure, in fact, whether the storm is really over. But one thing is certain. When you come out of the storm you won't be the same person who walked in. That's what this storm's all about.

Haruki Murakami

We like to think of our champions and our idols as superheroes who were born different from us. We don't like to think of them as relatively ordinary people who made themselves extraordinary.

Carol Dweck

Do one thing every day that scares you.

Mary Schmich

Difficult things take a long time, impossible things a little longer.

André A. Jackson

I remember one morning when I discovered a cocoon in the back of a tree just as a butterfly was making a hole in its case and preparing to come out. I waited awhile, but it was too long appearing and I was impatient. I bent over it and breathed on it to warm it. I warmed it as quickly as I could and the miracle began to happen before my eyes, faster than life. The case opened; the butterfly started slowly crawling out, and I shall never forget my horror when I saw how its wings were folded back and crumpled; the wretched butterfly tried with its whole trembling body to unfold them. Bending over it, I tried to help it with my breath, in vain.

It needed to be hatched out patiently and the unfolding of the wings should be a gradual process in the sun. Now it was too late. My breath had forced the butterfly to appear all crumpled, before its time. It struggled desperately and, a few seconds later, died in the palm of my hand.

That little body is, I do believe, the greatest weight I have on my conscience. For I realize today that it is a mortal sin to violate the great laws of nature. We should not hurry, we should not be impatient, but we should confidently obey the external rhythm.

Nikos Kazantzakis

Success doesn't come to you. You go to it.

Marva Collins

It always seems impossible, until it's done.

Nelson Mandela

Interviewer to William Faulkner: Some people say they can't understand your writing, even after they have read it two or three times. What approach would you suggest for them?

Faulkner: Read it four times.

Paris Review, 1956

All my work is meant to say, "You may encounter defeats, but you must not be defeated."

Maya Angelou

How can you teach people to be more creative? Give them harder problems.

Nelson Goodman

Winning is great, sure, but if you are really going to do something in life, the secret is learning how to lose. Nobody goes undefeated all the time. If you can pick up after a crushing defeat, and go on to win again, you are going to be a champion someday.

Wilma Rudolph

We have to believe that students can be successful with academic challenges the same way they are with character and physical challenges. . . .We can't wait until they are "ready," because what happens is that students in poverty and students at risk never even get to attempt that kind of work.

All students need the same access to academics that will prepare them for college and beyond.

Laurie Godwin

Look, disappointment and uncertainty are constant companions in life's pursuits. Being a little frightened is natural and unavoidable.

Sonia Sotomayor

Each difficult moment has the potential to open my eyes and open my heart.

Myla Kabat-Zinn

I really don't think life is about the I-could-have-beens. Life is only about the I-tried-to-do. I don't mind the failure but I can't imagine that I'd forgive myself if I didn't try.

Nikki Giovanni

Difficulties illuminate existence, but they must be fresh and of high quality.

Tom Robbins

Deeper instruction can be a powerful difference-maker in students' lives. A teacher's thoughtful intention to challenge, engage, and empower her students drives deeper learning and, in many cases students' investment in school. . .

A learning environment like this can transform how we feel about school and our futures as students, learners, and citizens.

From *Learning That Lasts*,
by Ron Berger, Libby Woodfin, Anne Vilen

It's not the load that breaks you down, it's the way you carry it.

Lena Horne

Sometimes the bravest and most important thing you can do is just show up.

Brene Brown

I have not failed. I've just found 10,000 ways that won't work.

Thomas Edison

Your disability is your opportunity.

Kurt Hahn

Walker, your footsteps
are the road, and nothing more.
Walker, there is no road,
the road is made by walking.

Antonio Machado

CHARACTER

Good teaching cannot be reduced to technique; good teaching comes from the identity and integrity of the teacher.

Parker Palmer

Courage doesn't always roar. Sometimes courage is the quiet voice at the end of the day saying, "I will try again tomorrow."

Mary Anne Radmacher

Remember when you go into the world to keep your eyes and ears wide open. And be kind. Love one another. Take care of each other. Tell the truth. Always do your best. Listen to the big people and the little people. Explore new paths and have fun. Know that you are loved like crazy. Give thanks for all your blessings. Above all else, love and you will do wonderful things in this world.

Rebecca Puig

We will be known forever by the tracks we leave.

Dakota Sioux proverb

Hold fast to dreams
For if dreams die
Life is a broken-winged bird
That cannot fly.

From "Dreams," by Langston Hughes

Long after students may have forgotten the historical names and dates they learned in class (which they will access online), they will flourish in college history classes and in life if their history teacher has imbued them with the life skills to be resilient, incisive thinkers and researchers; to have courage and integrity in expressing and critiquing ideas orally and in writing; and to have the skills to be an effective, collaborative worker.

From *Management in the Active Classroom*, by Ron Berger, Dina Strasser, Libby Woodfin

Every time someone gives you a formula for what you should be and what you should do, you should know they're giving you a pair of handcuffs.

Junot Díaz

"One of the first lines in the original [Expeditionary Learning] grant proposal was that we hold academic achievement on equal footing as character development. And that is true to this day."

Diana Lam

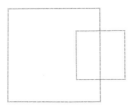

When we started our project, we thought that we were going to change our city. But what we really did is change ourselves. What we learned is that this kind of work takes strength, perseverance, and persistence. If things are going to be better, each of us, all citizens of the United States, need to BE the people.

Student, Polaris Charter Academy

Instead of hating the people you think are war-makers, hate the appetites and disorder in your own soul, which are the causes of war. If you love peace, then hate injustice, hate tyranny, hate greed —but hate these things in yourself, not in another.

Thomas Merton

[Daddy] said: "All children must look after their own upbringing." Parents can only give good advice or put them on the right paths, but the final forming of a person's character lies in their own hands.

Anne Frank

If we do not act, we shall surely be dragged down the long, dark and shameful corridors of time reserved for those who possess power without compassion, might without morality, and strength without sight.

Dr. Martin Luther King, Jr.

I change myself, I change the world.

Gloria Anzaldua

We who lived in concentration camps can remember the men who walked through the huts comforting others, giving away their last piece of bread. They may have been few in number, but they offer sufficient proof that everything can be taken from a man but one thing: the last of the human freedoms—to choose one's attitude in any given set of circumstances, to choose one's own way.

Viktor E. Frankl

A person is a person because he recognizes others as persons.

Desmond Tutu

People are just as wonderful as sunsets if you let them be. When I look at a sunset, I don't find myself saying, "Soften the orange a bit on the right hand corner." I don't try to control a sunset. I watch with awe as it unfolds.

Carl Rogers

If you treat an individual as he is, he will remain how he is. But if you treat him as if he were what he ought to be and could be, he will become what he ought to be and could be.

Johann Wolfgang von Goethe

Unless you choose to do great things with it, it makes no difference how much you are rewarded, or how much power you have.

Oprah Winfrey

When a person doesn't have gratitude, something is missing in his or her humanity. A person can almost be defined by his or her attitude toward gratitude.

Elie Wiesel

When people shine a little light on their monster, we find out how similar most of our monsters are. The secrecy, the obfuscation, the fact that these monsters can only be hinted at, gives us the sense that they must be very bad indeed. But when people let their monsters out for a little onstage interview, it turns out that we've all done or thought the same things, that this is our lot, our condition. We don't end up with a brand on our forehead. Instead, we compare notes.

Anne Lamott

We don't see things as they are.
We see things as we are.

Anais Nin

I've learned that people will forget what you said,
people will forget what you did, but people will
never forget how you made them feel.

Carl W. Buehner

I regard it as the foremost task of education
to insure the survival of these qualities: an
enterprising curiosity, an undefeatable spirit,
tenacity in pursuit, readiness for sensible self
denial, and above all, compassion.

The experience of helping a fellow man in danger,
or even training in a realistic manner to be able
to give this help, tends to change the balance of
power in a youth's inner life with the result that
compassion can be the master motive.

Kurt Hahn

It is not the brains that matter most, but that
which guides them—the character, the heart,
generous qualities, progressive ideas.

Fyodor Dostoyevsky

You are the sky—everything else—it's just the weather.

Pema Chodron

Love takes off the masks that we fear we cannot
live without and know we cannot live within.
I use the word "love" here not merely in the
personal sense but as a state of being, or a state
of grace—not in the infantile American sense of
being made happy but in the tough and universal
sense of quest and daring and growth.

James Baldwin

We are our choices.

Jean-Paul Sartre

It's really a wonder that I haven't dropped
all my ideals, because they seem so absurd
and impossible to carry out. Yet I keep them,
because in spite of everything I still believe that
people are really good at heart. I simply can't
build up my hopes on a foundation consisting
of confusion, misery, and death. I see the world
gradually being turned into a wilderness, I
hear the ever approaching thunder, which
will destroy us too, I can feel the sufferings of
millions and yet, if I look up into the heavens, I
think that it will all come right, that this cruelty
too will end, and that peace and tranquillity will
return again.

Anne Frank

"What is REAL?" asked the Rabbit one day, when they were lying side by side near the nursery fender, before Nana came to tidy the room. "Does it mean having things that buzz inside you and a stick-out handle?"

"Real isn't how you are made," said the Skin Horse. "It's a thing that happens to you. When a child loves you for a long, long time, not just to play with, but REALLY loves you, then you become Real."

"Does it hurt?" asked the Rabbit.

"Sometimes," said the Skin Horse, for he was always truthful. "When you are Real you don't mind being hurt."

"Does it happen all at once, like being wound up," he asked, "or bit by bit?"

"It doesn't happen all at once," said the Skin Horse. "You become. It takes a long time. That's why it doesn't happen often to people who break easily, or have sharp edges, or who have to be carefully kept. Generally, by the time you are Real, most of your hair has been loved off, and your eyes drop out and you get loose in the joints and very shabby. But these things don't matter at all, because once you are Real you can't be ugly, except to people who don't understand."

From *The Velveteen Rabbit*, by Margery Williams Bianco

THE GOLDEN RULE, ACROSS WORLD RELIGIONS:

HINDUISM
This is the sum of duty: do not do to others what would cause pain if done to you. (Mahabharata: 5:1517)

BUDDHISM
Hurt not others in ways that you yourself would find hurtful. (Udana-Varga 5.18)

CONFUCIANISM
Surely it is the maxim of loving-kindness: Do not unto others what you would not have them do unto you. (Analects 15:23)

TAOISM
Regard your neighbor's gain as your own gain, and your neighbor's loss as your own loss. (Tai Shang Kan Ying P'ien, 213-218)

JUDAISM
What is hateful to you, do not to your neighbor. This is the entire Law; all the rest is commentary." (Talmud, Shabbat 31a)

CHRISTIANITY
In everything, do to others as you would have them do to you; for this is the law and the prophets (Matthew 7:12)

ISLAM
Not one of you truly believes until you wish for others what you wish for yourself (Sunnah)

CRAFTSMANSHIP

We believe that every student, every student, wants to contribute things of value to the world.

Ron Berger

There are several ways to perform almost any act—an efficient, workable, artistic way and a careless, indifferent, sloppy way. Care and artistry are worth the trouble. They can be a satisfaction to the practitioner and a joy to all beholders.

Helen Nearing

If you are irritated by every rub, how will you be polished?

Rumi

When a work lifts your spirits and inspires bold and noble thoughts in you, do not look for any other standard to judge by: the work is good, the product of a master craftsman.

Jean de la Bruyere

Insisting on high-quality work is an indisputable message that teachers care about their students and believe they are capable and worthy.

Sonia Nieto

The most important assessments that take place in any school building are seen by no one. They take place inside the heads of students, all day long. Students assess what they do, say, and produce, and decide what is good enough. These internal assessments govern how much they care, how hard they work, and how much they learn. They govern how kind and polite they are and how respectful and responsible. They set the standard for what is "good enough" in class. In the end, these are the assessments that really matter. All other assessments are in service of this goal—to get inside students' heads and raise the bar for effort and quality.

From *Leaders of Their Own Learning*,
by Ron Berger, Leah Rugen, Libby Woodfin

Develop craftsmanship through years of wide reading.

Annie Proulx

A person who knows how to fix motorcycles...with Quality...is less likely to run short of friends than one who doesn't. And they aren't going to see him as some kind of object either. Quality destroys objectivity every time.

Or if he takes whatever dull job he's stuck with... and they are all, sooner or later, dull...and, just to keep himself amused, starts to look for options of Quality, and secretly pursues these options, just for their own sake, thus making an art out of what he is doing, he's likely to discover that he becomes a much more interesting person and much less of an object to the people around him because his Quality decisions change him too. And not only the job and him, but others too because the Quality tends to fan out like waves. The Quality job he didn't think anyone was going to see is seen, and the person who sees it feels a little better because of it, and is likely to pass that feeling on to others, and in that way the Quality tends to keep on going.

Robert Pirsig

Celebrate what you want to see more of.

Tom Peters

Craftsmanship isn't like water in an earthen pot, to be taken out by the dipperful until it's empty. No, the more drawn out the more remains.

Lloyd Alexander

If you are going to do something, I believe, you should do it well. You should sweat over it and make sure it's strong and accurate and beautiful and you should be proud of it. In carpentry, there is no higher compliment builders give each other than this: That person is a craftsman... I want a classroom full of craftsmen. I want students whose work is strong and accurate and beautiful. Students who are proud of what they do, proud of how they respect themselves and others.

From *An Ethic of Excellence*, by Ron Berger

If you have no critics you'll likely have no success.

Malcolm X

"Do you understand how there could be any writing in a spider's web?"

"Oh, no," said Dr. Dorian. "I don't understand it. But for that matter I don't understand how a spider learned to spin a web in the first place. When the words appeared, everyone said they were a miracle. But nobody pointed out that the web itself is a miracle."

From *Charlotte's Web*, by E.B. White

Anyone who has never made a mistake has never tried anything new.

Albert Einstein

Nobody sees a flower, really, it is so small. We haven't time—and to see takes time like to have a friend takes time.

If I could paint the flower exactly as I see it no one would see what I see because I would paint it small like the flower is small. So I said to myself, I'll paint what I see—what the flower is to me but I'll paint it big and they will be surprised into taking time to look at it—I will make even busy New Yorkers take time to see what I see of flowers.

Georgia O'Keeffe

CREW

On a boat, passengers are catered to. Their main purpose is to arrive at the destination with as little effort as possible. They are involved in activities, but not wholly engaged in the journey. Crew, on the other hand, are responsible for the entire journey. They are engrossed in the activities of the ship. In fact, without their individual and collaborative effort, the passage cannot happen. Crew reach the same destination as their passengers, but their experience is significantly richer.

Author unknown

I believe that it's almost impossible for people to change alone. We need to join with others who will push us in our thinking and challenge us to do things we didn't believe ourselves capable of.

Frances Moore Lappe

You can't motivate a student you don't know.

Ted Sizer

Ubuntu is very difficult to render into a Western language. It speaks of the very essence of being human... You share what you have. It is to say, 'My humanity is caught up, is inextricably bound up, in yours.' We belong in a bundle of life. We say, 'A person is a person through other persons.' It is not, 'I think, therefore I am.' It says rather, 'I am human because I belong. I participate. I share.' A person with ubuntu is open and available to others, affirming of others, does not feel threatened that others are able and good, for he or she has a proper self-assurance that comes from knowing that he or she belongs in a greater whole and is diminished when others are humiliated or diminished, when others are tortured or oppressed, or treated as if they were less than who they are.

Desmond Tutu

I want, by understanding myself, to understand others. I want to be all that I am capable of becoming.

Katherine Mansfield

No significant learning occurs without a significant relationship.

James Comer

The world is so empty if one thinks only of mountains, rivers and cities; but to know someone who thinks and feels with us, and who, though distant, is close to us in spirit, this makes the earth for us an inhabited garden.

Johann Wolfgang von Goethe

Empathy is a strange and powerful thing. There is no script. There is no right way or wrong way to do it. It's simply listening, holding space, withholding judgement, emotionally connecting, and communicating that incredibly healing message of "you are not alone."

Brene Brown

Every person that you meet knows something you don't; learn from them.

H. Jackson Brown Jr.

How are we to find our way toward conversation? For me, the answer has always been through story. Story bypasses rhetoric and pierces the heart. Story offers a wash of images and emotion that returns us to our highest and deepest selves, where we remember what it means to be human, living in a place with our neighbors.

Terry Tempest Williams

Trust, however, is not the same thing as warmth, happiness, familiarity, kindness. These are all wonderful qualities—and trusting communities usually include them—but trust is something different. When you have repeated evidence that your colleagues respectfully say what they think, tell you directly to your face when they disagree, and say honestly when they don't know something, you begin to trust them a whole lot more than when you were just exchanging niceties.

Sarah Fiarman

Most of the time, all you have is the moment, and the imperfect love of the people around you.

Anne Lamott

One of the oldest human needs is having someone to wonder where you are when you don't come home at night.

Margaret Mead

One finger cannot lift a pebble.

Hopi proverb

Why circles? They are egalitarian and invite participation. They allow everyone to see and hear everyone else, unfettered by furniture or belongings. They allow greater access to our hearts and bodies, not just our heads. Circles are an ancient way to gather and share in a way that supports connection.

Cyndi Gueswel

LESSONS FROM GEESE

FACT 1

As each goose flaps its wings, it creates an "uplift" for the birds that follow. By flying in a "V" formation, the whole flock has 71% greater flying range than if each bird flew alone.

LESSON

People who share a common direction and sense of community can get where they are going faster and more easily, because they are traveling on each other's effort and momentum.

FACT 2

When a goose falls out of formation, it suddenly feels the drag and resistance of flying alone. It quickly moves back into formation to take advantage of the lifting power of the bird immediately in front of it.

LESSON

If we have as much sense as a goose, we stay in formation with those headed where we want to go. We are willing to accept their help and give our help to others.

FACT 3

When the lead bird tires, it rotates back into the formation to take advantage of the lifting power of the bird immediately in front of it.

LESSON

It pays to take turns doing the hard tasks and sharing leadership. As with geese, people are interdependent on each others' skills, capabilities, and unique arrangement of gifts, talents, and resources.

FACT 4

The geese flying in formation honk to encourage those up front to keep up their speed.

LESSON

We need to make sure our honking is encouraging. In groups where there is encouragement, the production is much greater. The power of encouragement is the quality of honking we seek.

FACT 5

When a goose gets sick, wounded, or shot down, two geese drop out of formation and follow it down to help and protect it. They stay with it until it dies or is able to fly again. Then, they launch out with another formation to catch up with the flock.

LESSON

If we have as much sense as geese, we will stand by each other in difficult times as well as when we're strong. The collective commitment of the group creates security for each individual.

Adapted from the original written by Robert McNeish

ALLEGORY OF THE LONG SPOONS

People are always wishing. But once in China a man got his wish, which was to see the difference between heaven and hell before he died. When he visited hell, he saw tables crowded with delicious food, but everyone was hungry and angry. They had food, but were forced to sit several feet from the table and use spoons three feet long that made it impossible to get any food into their mouths.

When the man saw heaven, he was very surprised for it looked the same. Big tables of delicious food. People forced to sit several feet from the table and use three-foot long spoons that made it impossible to get any food into their mouths. It was exactly like hell, but in heaven the people were well-fed and happy.

Why?

In heaven, they were feeding one another.

Author unknown

ENGAGEMENT

The idea is to put together really important and difficult work with great joy in doing it.

Greg Farrell

Philosophers have long conceded, however, that every man has two educations: 'that which is given to him, and that which he gives himself. Of the two kinds the latter is by far the more desirable. Indeed all that is most worthy in man he must work out and conquer for himself. It is that which constitutes our real and best nourishment. What we are merely taught seldom nourishes the mind like that which we teach ourselves.

Carter Woodson

To know how much there is to know is the beginning of learning to live.

Dorothy West

It is not true that people stop pursuing dreams because they grow old, they grow old because they stop pursuing dreams.

Gabriel García Márquez

We must dare, in the full sense of the word, to speak of love without fear of being called ridiculous, mawkish, or unscientific, if not antiscientific. We must dare in order to say scientifically, and not as mere blah-blah- blah, that we study, we learn, we teach, we know with our entire body. We do all of these things with feeling, with emotion, with wishes, with fear, with doubts, with passion, and also critical reasoning. However, we never study, learn, teach, or know with the last only. We must dare so as never to dichotomize cognition and emotion.

Paulo Freire

Students deserve to read beautifully written and worthy texts. If it is literature, let it be great literature. If it is informational text, let it teach students new words and new ideas in sophisticated ways. Let it, always, be worth their time and effort to read.

From *Your Curriculum Companion*,
by Libby Woodfin and Suzanne Plaut

We can choose to be a character in a story written out by someone else or we can choose to be the author of our own story.

Ruby Garcia

I decided to start anew—to strip away what I had been taught—to accept as true my own thinking. This was one of the best times of my life. There was no one around to look at what I was doing—no one interested—no one to say anything about it one way or another. I was alone and singularly free, working into my own, unknown—no one to satisfy but myself. I began with charcoal and paper and decided not to use any color until it was impossible to do what I wanted to do in black and white. I believe it was June before I needed blue.

Georgia O'Keefe

Sell your cleverness and buy bewilderment.

Rumi

For too long, school was something that was "done to kids" rather than having kids be leaders of their own learning. Teachers like us have changed that notion, and we are helping thousands of kids realize that their voices deserve to be heard, that they, too, have choice and agency, and that they can be the change they want to see in the world.

Chris Dolgos

The most beautiful thing we can experience is the mysterious. It is the source of all true art and science. He to whom this emotion is a stranger, who can no longer pause to wonder and stand rapt in awe, is as good as dead: his eyes are closed.

Albert Einstein

Values must be clear and the value of values clearly demonstrable; there is no learning without emotion and challenge; it must be done with intimacy and caring; the collective and the individual can be brought together; there must be a fair assurance of success.

Paul Ylvisaker

Exhaust the little moment. Soon it dies.
And be it gash or gold it will not come
Again in this identical disguise.

Gwendolyn Brooks

Travel light and travel simple, in your mind, through your world. I think that leaving spaces for things that you haven't planned is the real secret to life. You shouldn't pack yourself in too tightly. Above all, you have to leave room in life to dream.

Buffy Sainte-Marie

What makes life worth living?

No child asks itself that question. To children life is self-evident. Life goes without saying: whether it is good or bad makes no difference. This is because children don't see the world, don't observe the world, don't contemplate the world, but are so deeply immersed in the world that they don't distinguish between it and their own selves. Not until that happens, until a distance appears between what they are and what the world is, does the question arise: what makes life worth living?

Karl Ove Knausgaard

In the beginner's mind there are many possibilities, in the expert's mind there are few.

Shunryu Suzuki

In many shamanic societies, if you came to a medicine person complaining of being disheartened, dispirited, or depressed, they would ask one of four questions: When did you stop dancing? When did you stop singing? When did you stop being enchanted with stories? When did you stop finding comfort in the sweet territory of silence?

Gabrielle Roth

The marvelous thing about a good question is that it shapes our identity as much by the asking as it does by the answering. Therefore, at any time of life, follow your own questions; don't mistake other people's questions for your own.

David Whyte

And the day came when the risk it took to remain tight inside the bud was more painful than the risk it took to blossom.

Elizabeth Appell

I beg you... as well as I can, to have patience with everything unresolved in your heart and to try to love the questions themselves as if they were locked rooms or books written in a very foreign language. Don't search for the answers, which could not be given to you now, because you would not be able to live them. And the point is to live everything. Live the questions now. Perhaps then, someday far in the future, you will gradually, without even noticing it, live your way into the answer.

Rainer Maria Rilke

Once you wake up thought in a man, you can never put it to sleep again.

Zora Neale Hurston

[If you want to build a boat...] One will weave the canvas; another will fell a tree by the light of his ax. Yet another will forge nails, and there will be others who observe the stars to learn how to navigate. And yet all will be as one. Building a boat isn't about weaving canvas, forging nails, or reading the sky. It's about giving a shared taste for the sea, by the light of which you will see nothing contradictory but rather a community of love.

Antoine de Saint-Exupery

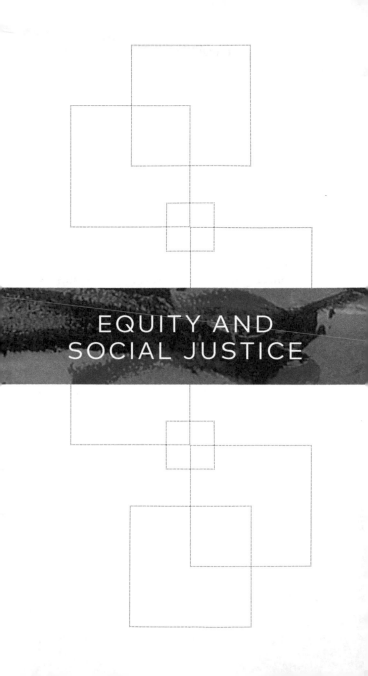

EQUITY AND
SOCIAL JUSTICE

It is not our differences that divide us. It is our inability to recognize, accept, and celebrate those differences.

Audre Lorde

Where you see wrong or inequality or injustice, speak out, because this is your country. This is your democracy. Make it. Protect it. Pass it on.

Thurgood Marshall

We only need enough courage to invite friends into a conversation. Large and successful change efforts start with conversations among friends, not with those in power. "Some friends and I started talking..." Change doesn't happen from a leader announcing the plan. Change begins from deep inside a system, when a few people notice something they will no longer tolerate, or respond to a dream of what's possible. We just have to find a few others who care about the same thing. Together we will figure out what our first step is, then the next, then the next. Gradually, we become large and powerful. We don't have to start with power, only with passion.

Margaret Wheatley

Education is education. We should learn everything and then choose which path to follow. Education is neither Eastern nor Western, it is human.

Malala Yousafzai

In every position that I've been in, there have been naysayers who don't believe I'm qualified or who don't believe I can do the work. And I feel a special responsibility to prove them wrong.

Sonia Sotomayor

True peace is not merely the absence of tension; it is the presence of justice."

Dr. Martin Luther King, Jr.

Schools should have courageous conversations like Casco Bay does. If they gained the same support that I and my friends did, that might influence their mind to influence others not to do what that young adult did (a hate crime) and that would just make the world a little more peaceful.

Atak Natali, Casco Bay High School student who was targeted in a racial hate crime

If you are neutral in situations of injustice, you have chosen the side of the oppressor. If an elephant has its foot on the tail of a mouse, and you say that you are neutral, the mouse will not appreciate your neutrality.

Desmond Tutu

When those who have the power to name and to socially construct reality choose not to see you or hear you...when someone with the authority of a teacher, say, describes the world and you are not in it, there is a moment of psychic disequilibrium, as if you looked in the mirror and saw nothing. It takes some strength of soul—and not just individual strength, but collective understanding—to resist this void, this non-being, into which you are thrust, and to stand up, demanding to be seen and heard.

Adrienne Rich

History, despite its wrenching pain
Cannot be unlived, but if faced
With courage, need not be lived again.

Maya Angelou

Once you learn to read, you will be forever free.

Frederick Douglass

For me, forgiveness and compassion are always linked: how do we hold people accountable for wrongdoing and yet at the same time remain in touch with their humanity enough to believe in their capacity to be transformed?

bell hooks

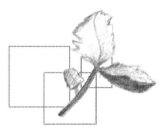

We cannot seek achievement for ourselves and forget about progress and prosperity for our community... Our ambitions must be broad enough to include the aspirations and needs of others, for their sakes and for our own.

Cesar Chavez

Love and justice are not two. Without inner change, there can be no outer change. Without collective change, no change matters.

Angel Kyodo Williams

If I love you, I have to make you conscious of the things that you don't see.

James Baldwin

If you have come to help me you are wasting your time. But if you recognize that your liberation and mine are bound up together, we can walk together.

Aboriginal activists group, Queensland, Australia

No one is born hating another person because of the color of his skin, or his background, or his religion. People must learn to hate, and if they can learn to hate, they can be taught to love, for love comes more naturally to the human heart than its opposite.

Nelson Mandela

BELLING THE CAT

Long ago, the mice had a general council to consider what measures they could take to outwit their common enemy, the Cat. Some said this, and some said that; but at last a young mouse got up and said he had a proposal to make, which he thought would meet the case. "You will all agree," said he, "that our chief danger consists in the sly and treacherous manner in which the enemy approaches us. Now, if we could receive some signal of her approach, we could easily escape from her. I venture, therefore, to propose that a small bell be procured, and attached by a ribbon around the neck of the Cat. By this means we should always know when she was about, and could easily retire while she was in the neighborhood.

This proposal met with general applause, until an old mouse got up and said: "That is all very well, but who is to bell the Cat?" The mice looked at one another and nobody spoke.

Aesop

Prejudice is one of the inescapable consequences of living in a racist society... [It] is like smog in the air. Sometimes it is so thick it is visible, other times it is less apparent, but always, day in and day out, we are breathing it in. None of us would introduce ourselves as "smog-breathers" (and most of us don't want to be described as prejudiced), but if we live in a smoggy place, how can we avoid breathing the air?

....We may not have polluted the air, but we need to take responsibility, along with others, for cleaning it up. Each of us needs to look at our own behavior.

Beverly Daniel Tatum

If you're walking down the right path and you're willing to keep walking, eventually you'll make progress.

President Barack Obama

If there is no struggle, there is no progress. Those who profess to favor freedom, and to depreciate agitation, are those who want crops without plowing up the ground.

Frederick Douglass

To wrench anything out of its accustomed course takes energy, effort, and pain. It does great violence to the existing pattern. Many people want change, various types of change, both in the external world and in their own internal world, but they are unwilling to undergo the severe hurt, the incredible pain that must precede it.

The only peaceful change is surface change— powdery snow blowing off the ice-hard earth.

I have read that rivers in extremely cold climates freeze over in winter. In the spring, when they thaw, the sound of ice cracking is an incredibly violent sound. The more extensive and severe the freeze, the more thunderous the thaw. Yet, at the end of the cracking, breaking, violent period, the river is open, life-giving, life-carrying. No one says, "Let's not suffer all the violence of the thaw; let's keep the freeze; at least everything is quiet then, unmoving, unchanging." No, after the winter is over, when it is time, people want change; they want the ice to melt and are willing to endure the violence that accompanies it.

Mary Mebane

If we are to achieve a richer culture, rich in contrasting values, we must recognize the whole gamut of human potentialities, and so weave a less arbitrary social fabric, one in which each diverse human gift will find a fitting place.

Margaret Mead

What the best and wisest parent wants for his own child, that must the community want for all of its children. Any other ideal for our schools in narrow and unlovely; acted upon, it destroys our democracy.

John Dewey

In contrast to civic readiness, the goal of college readiness for all students is a relatively new goal for our country. For most of our history, the goal of college readiness applied to a small elite group of students; all others were prepared for basic skills in life and work. Schools were designed to sort students and prepare them for their different roles. Although college may not be the path that every student takes, every student deserves to be prepared to make that choice and to be privileged with challenging academic preparation.

From *Transformational Literacy*, by Ron Berger, Libby Woodfin, Suzanne Plaut, and Cheryl Dobbertin

No country can ever truly flourish if it stifles the potential of its women and deprives itself of the contributions of half of its citizens.

Michelle Obama

A thread running from Plato through Hahn and through Outward Bound is the responsibility of individuals to make their own personal goals consonant with social necessity. Not only is the part subordinated to the whole, but the part cannot even understand its own identity, its relations and its responsibility, until it has grasped the nature of the whole.

Tom James

LEADERSHIP

School reform, by its very nature, requires a sustained effort. It takes more time to improve schools than is generally discussed or acknowledged in the press and in political debate, and it takes longer than our political structures support. Ideas are important, but they come in a moment. Doing is what counts, and doing takes years. "If you want to change schools," one superintendent-reformer told me—in 1964—"learn to grow trees."

Leaders have to provide a focus: Choose a direction and stick to it. They have to be reliable and persistent. For school reform to succeed, we, and especially the leaders, have to keep tending the trees. With respect to the work of improving schools and student achievement, leaders do not accomplish much if they are not there for the long haul. Trust and time are the fundamental requirements for growing good schools. Trust is built through constancy. Constancy is demonstrated over time.

Greg Farrell

Go to the people. Live with them. Learn from them. Love them. Start with what they know. Build with what they have. But with the best leaders, when the work is done, the task accomplished, the people will say "We have done this ourselves."

Lao Tzu

Leaders who live in the new story help us understand ourselves differently by the way they lead. They trust our humanness; they welcome the surprises we bring to them; they are curious about our differences; they delight in our inventiveness; they nurture us; they connect us. They trust that we can create wisely and well, that we seek the best interests of our organization and community, that we want to bring more good into the world.

Margaret Wheatley

It is better to have less thunder in the mouth and more lightning in the hand.

Apache proverb

Leadership is about making others better as a result of your presence and making sure that impact lasts in your absence.

Sheryl Sandberg

Tune your body to the mountain, to the distance you have to go. Take a pace you can keep up all day.

Tap Tapley

The most effective way to do it, is to do it.

Amelia Earhart

Change will not come if we wait for some other person, or if we wait for some other time. We are the ones we've been waiting for. We are the change that we seek.

President Barack Obama

The key is to keep tinkering toward better, to keep loving your students, and to mine the wisdom they already have.

Derek Pierce

Leadership is scarce because few people are willing to go through the discomfort required to lead. This scarcity makes leadership valuable...It's uncomfortable to stand up in front of strangers. It's uncomfortable to propose an idea that might fail. It's uncomfortable to challenge the status quo. It's uncomfortable to resist the urge to settle. When you identify the discomfort, you've found the place where a leader is needed. If you are not uncomfortable in your work as a leader, it's almost certain you're not reaching your potential as a leader.

Seth Godin

When others are complaining, you're imagining solutions.

Marsha Ratzel

What focus means is saying no to something that you, with every bone in your body, you think is a phenomenal idea, and you wake up thinking about it, but you say no to it because you're focusing on something else.

Jony Ive

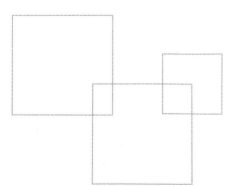

Don't cling to a mistake just because you spent a lot of time making it.

Aubrey De Graf

We're used to thinking of a school as a unified organization—"That's a good school. That one isn't so good." In fact, research shows that there tends to be more variation within a single school than across different schools. So a principal's job isn't to take a bad school and make it good. Rather, the challenge is to make a school more consistently effective across all classrooms. To create a school that is not a collection of separate teaching units but an internally coherent organization unified by a set of best practices.

Sarah Fiarman

We cannot see our reflection in running water. It is only in still water that we can see.

Zen saying

I've come to a frightening conclusion that I am the decisive element in the classroom. It's my personal approach that creates the climate. It's my daily mood that makes the weather. As a teacher, I possess a tremendous power to make a child's life miserable or joyous. I can be a tool of torture or an instrument of inspiration. I can humiliate or heal. In all situations, it is my response that decides whether a crisis will be escalated or de-escalated and a child humanized or dehumanized.

Haim Ginott

No matter what, expect the unexpected, and whenever possible, BE the unexpected.

Lynda Barry

I am only one, but still I am one. I cannot do everything, but still I can do something; and because I cannot do everything, I will not refuse to do the something that I can do.

Edward Everett Hale

When I dare to be powerful, to use my strength in the service of my vision, then it becomes less and less important whether I am afraid.

Audre Lorde

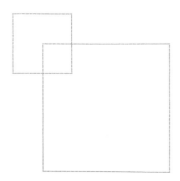

THE BIG ROCKS OF LIFE

One day this expert was speaking to a group of business students and, to drive home a point, used an illustration I'm sure those students will never forget. After I share it with you, you'll never forget it either.

As this man stood in front of the group of high-powered over-achievers he said, "Okay, time for a quiz." Then he pulled out a one-gallon, wide-mouthed mason jar and set it on a table in front of him. Then he produced about a dozen fist-sized rocks and carefully placed them, one at a time, into the jar.

When the jar was filled to the top and no more rocks would fit inside, he asked, "Is this jar full?" Everyone in the class said, "Yes." Then he said, "Really?" He reached under the table and pulled out a bucket of gravel. Then he dumped some gravel in and shook the jar causing pieces of gravel to work themselves down into the spaces between the big rocks.

Then he smiled and asked the group once more, "Is the jar full?" By this time the class was onto him. "Probably not," one of them answered. "Good!" he replied. And he reached under the table and brought out a bucket of sand. He started dumping the sand in and it went into all the spaces left between the rocks and the gravel. Once more he asked the question, "Is this jar full?"

"No!" the class shouted. Once again he said, "Good!" Then he grabbed a pitcher of water and began to pour it in until the jar was filled to the brim. Then he looked up at the class and asked, "What is the point of this illustration?"

One eager beaver raised his hand and said, "The point is, no matter how full your schedule is, if you try really hard, you can always fit some more things into it!"

"No," the speaker replied, "that's not the point. The truth this illustration teaches us is: If you don't put the big rocks in first, you'll never get them in at all."

Steven Covey

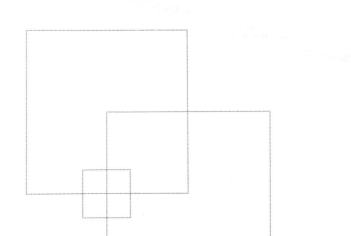

NATURE
AND ADVENTURE

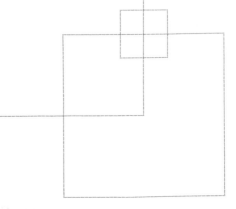

Instructions for living a life:
Pay attention.
Be astonished.
Tell about it.

From "Sometimes," by Mary Oliver

You don't climb mountains without a team, you don't climb mountains without being fit, you don't climb mountains without being prepared and you don't climb mountains without balancing the risks and rewards. And you never climb a mountain on accident—it has to be intentional.

Mark Udall

He had missed the deepest of all companionships, a relation with the earth itself, with a countryside and a people. That relationship, he knew, cannot be gone after and found; it must be long and deliberate, unconscious. It must, indeed, be a way of living...and he had begun to believe it the most satisfying tie men can have.

Willa Cather

Those who dwell among the beauties and mysteries of the earth are never alone or weary of life....Those who contemplate the beauty of the earth find reserves of strength that will endure as long as life lasts.

Rachel Carson

Always in the big woods when you leave familiar ground and step off alone into a new place there will be, along with the feelings of curiosity and excitement, a little nagging of dread. It is the ancient fear of the Unknown, and it is your first bond with the wilderness you are going into. What you are doing is exploring. You are undertaking the first experience, not of the place, but of yourself in that place. It is an experience of essential loneliness; for nobody can discover the world for anybody else. It is only after we have discovered it for ourselves that it becomes a common ground and bond, and we cease to be alone.

Wendell Berry

People from a planet without flowers would think we must be mad with joy the whole time to have such things about us.

Iris Murdoch

The eyes of the future are looking back at us and they are praying for us to see beyond our own time. They are kneeling with hands clasped that we might act with restraint, that we might leave room for the life that is destined to come. To protect what is wild is to protect what is gentle. Perhaps the wilderness we fear is the pause between our own heartbeats, the silent space that says we live only by grace. Wilderness lives by this same grace. Wild mercy is in our hands.

Terry Tempest Williams

Even if we manage to stand upon the summit, I now realize that this will be only a small part of what I gain from this adventure. The real power of setting distant goals lies not in the moment of attainment, but in the exploring of new worlds that are cast open to those who are willing to make the journey...Pumori's gift was to provide a dream worthy of chasing into worlds far away.

Scott Hartl

....

You never conquer a mountain.
You stand on the summit a few moments;
Then the wind blows your footprints away.

Arlene Blum

....

You do not have to sit outside in the dark. If, however, you want to look at the stars, you will find that darkness is necessary. But the stars neither require nor demand it.

Annie Dillard

....

She say, My first step from the old white man was trees. Then air. Then birds. Then other people. But one day when I was sitting quiet and feeling like a motherless child, which I was, it came to me: that feeling of being part of everything, not separate at all. I knew that if I cut a tree, my arm would bleed. And I laughed and I cried and I run all around the house. I just knew what it was. In fact, when it happen, you can't miss it.

From *The Color Purple*, by Alice Walker

LESSONS FROM THE SEA

Never be complacent. A lapse of attention, even for a moment, can have dire, or at least unpleasant consequences.

Travel light. Take care of what you have. Things last a lot longer than you ever imagined.

Comfort is relative. We adjust to our surroundings like the sense of smell. Monday's dirty laundry might be the cleanest thing you have on Thursday.

Who would have guessed you could rejoice at finding that perfectly contoured shell or velvet smooth stick? Beauty has nothing to do with Madison Avenue or Hollywood.

You have absolutely no control over the circumstances around you. All you can control is how you react. Plan carefully, read the signs, and adjust your course.

There is no such thing as standing still. If you are not active, you will drift off course.

To find your way, line up short term plans with long range goals.

Use your big muscles. Go with your strength.

....But finesse over strength whenever you can.

Some effort on the right turns you right. Some effort on the right turns you left. Know when to use your hands and when to use your feet.

Steven Levy

May your trails be crooked, winding, lonesome, dangerous, leading to the most amazing view. May your mountains rise into and above the clouds. May your rivers flow without end, meandering through pastoral valleys tinkling with bells, past temples and castles and poets' towers into a dark primeval forest where tigers belch and monkeys howl, through miasmal and mysterious swamps and down into a desert of red rock, blue mesas, domes and pinnacles and grottos of endless stone, and down again into a deep vast ancient unknown chasm where bars of sunlight blaze on profiled cliffs, where deer walk across the white sand beaches, where storms come and go as lightning clangs upon the high crags, where something strange and more beautiful and more full of wonder than your deepest dreams waits for you—beyond that next turning of the canyon walls.

Edward Abbey

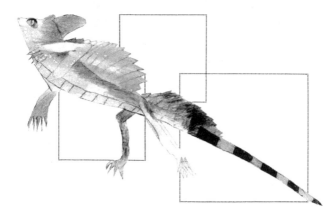

At around age six, perhaps, I was standing by myself in our front yard waiting for supper, just at that hour in a late summer day when the sun is already below the horizon and the risen full moon in the visible sky stops being chalky and begins to take on light. There comes the moment, and I saw it then, when the moon goes from flat to round. For the first time it met my eyes as a globe. The word 'moon' came into my mouth as though fed to me out of a silver spoon. Held in my mouth the moon became a word. It had the roundness of a Concord grape Grandpa took off his vine and gave me to suck out of its skin and swallow whole, in Ohio.

Eudora Welty

We know ourselves to be made from this earth. We know this earth is made from our bodies. For we see ourselves. And we are nature. We are nature seeing nature. We are nature with a concept of nature. Nature weeping. Nature speaking of nature to nature.

Susan Griffiin

Around the bend now came...two boys in a canoe.

What time is it?' was their first question. They explained that their watches had run down, and for the first time in their lives there was no clock, whistle, or radio to set watches by. For two days they had lived by 'sun-time,' and were getting a thrill out of it...No friendly roof kept them dry when they misguessed whether or not to pitch the tent. No guide showed them which camping spots offered a nightlong breeze, and which a nightlong misery of mosquitoes; which firewood made clean coals, and which only smoke.

...The elemental simplicities of wilderness travel were thrills not only because of their novelty, but because they represented complete freedom to make mistakes. The wilderness gave them their first taste of those rewards and penalties for wise and foolish acts which every woodsman faces daily, but against which civilization has built a thousand buffers.

Aldo Leopold

To see and know a place is a contemplative act. It means emptying our minds and letting what is there, in all its multiplicity and endless variety, come in.

Gretel Ehrlich

The more clearly we can focus our attention on the wonders and realities of the universe about us, the less taste we shall have for destruction.

Rachel Carson

And there at the camp, we had around us the elemental world of water and light, and earth and air. We felt the presences of the wild creatures, the river, the trees, the stars. Though we had our troubles, we had them in a true perspective.

The universe, as we could see any night, is unimaginably large, and mostly dark. We knew we needed to be together more than we needed to be apart.

Wendell Berry

SERVICE AND CONTRIBUTION

I will not die an unlived life. I will not live in fear of falling or catching fire. I choose to inhabit my days, to allow my living to open me, to make me less afraid, more accessible, to loosen my heart until it becomes a wing, a torch, a promise. I choose to risk my significance; to live so that which comes to me as seed goes to the next as blossom and that which comes to me as blossom, goes on as fruit.

Dawna Markova

A life is not important except in the impact it has on other lives.

Jackie Robinson

What if students went to school with a mission, not just to get smart, but also to become a better person, and contribute to a better world? School could be a place of compassion and courage, a place of hope. I am a high school student in Chicago. My neighborhood has challenges; poverty and violence make life difficult for many families. But I have a privileged life. My privilege doesn't come from money or safe streets. My privilege comes from attending a school with a different vision of what is possible. Our test scores are good, but that's not the most important thing. Our work is beautiful, but even that's not the most important thing. This is what's most important: we work together to get smart for a purpose, to make our community and the world a better place.

Ameerah Rollins, Student, Polaris Charter Academy

Attention is the rarest and purest form of generosity.

Simone Weil

....

We must not, in trying to think about how we
can make a big difference, ignore the small daily
differences we can make which, over time, add up
to big differences that we often cannot foresee.

Marian Wright Edelman

....

There are three ways of trying to win the young.
There is persuasion, there is compulsion, and there
is attraction. You can preach at them: that is a hook
without a worm. You can say, You must volunteer,
and that is of the devil. You can tell them, You are
needed. That appeal hardly ever fails.

Kurt Hahn

....

To affect the quality of the day, that is
the highest of arts.

Henry David Thoreau

SERVICE AND CONTRIBUTION

With this new paradigm [where service-learning is integral to the mission and practice of higher education]...we would see students not as empty vessels to be filled with knowledge but as active learners who build meaning through context. We would see the campus not as an ivory tower, but as a socially engaged institution. We would see community service not as charity, but as reciprocal process with reciprocal benefits. We would see teaching and research not only as the domain of faculty, but also as the work of students and community partners...we would see education not as a value-free venture, but as a directional process cultivating public virtues and meeting public needs.

Goodwin Liu

Love is an action, never simply a feeling.

bell hooks

Students are not learning to be citizens someday. They are citizens now.

Reggio Emilia Schools

The work of the world is common as mud.
Botched, it smears the hands, crumbles to dust.
But the thing worth doing well done
has a shape that satisfies, clean and evident.
Greek amphoras for wine or oil,
Hopi vases that held corn, are put in museums
but you know they were made to be used.

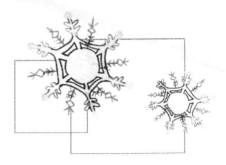

The pitcher cries for water to carry
and a person for work that is real.

From "To Be of Use," by Marge Piercy

If you think you are too small to be effective, you
have never been in bed with a mosquito.

Betty Reese

Service is the Grand Canyon of character
development.

Meg Campbell

Our deepest fear is not that we are inadequate.
Our deepest fear is that we are powerful beyond
measure. It is our light, not our darkness that most
frightens us. We ask ourselves, Who am I to be
brilliant, gorgeous, talented, fabulous? Actually,
who are you not to be? You are a child of God.
Your playing small does not serve the world.
There is nothing enlightened about shrinking
so that other people won't feel insecure around

you. We are all meant to shine, as children do. We were born to make manifest the glory of God that is within us. It's not just in some of us; it's in everyone. And as we let our own light shine, we unconsciously give other people permission to do the same. As we are liberated from our own fear, our presence automatically liberates others.

Marianne Williamson

The critical insight of EL Education is that belonging alone is not enough. In order for a student to feel truly motivated by and about school, he also has to perceive that he is doing important work—work that is challenging, rigorous and deep.

Paul Tough

I had been my whole life a bell, and never knew it until at that moment I was lifted and struck.

Annie Dillard

Tell me, what is it you plan to do with your one wild and precious life?

From "The Summer Day," by Mary Oliver

We automatically give to each person we meet, but we choose what we give. Our words, our actions, must consciously set the stage for the life we wish to lead.

Marlo Morgan

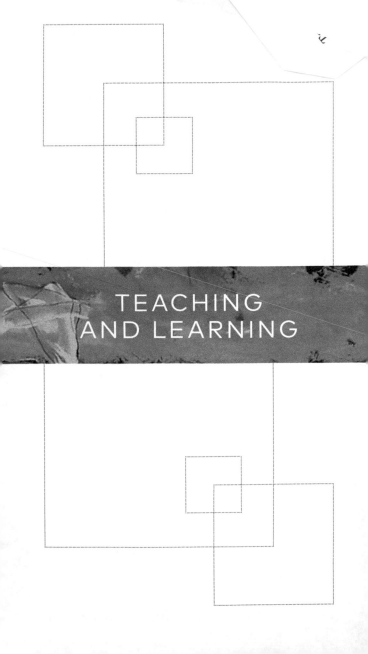

TEACHING
AND LEARNING

start a school is to proclaim what it means to be a human being. Depending on the time and the place, the message can be somewhat obvious and comfortable or startling and radically unsettling. If we are to be true to ourselves and true to learning today, we must prepare for the latter.

Tom James

....

...if I had to put a finger on what I consider a good education, a good radical education, it wouldn't be anything about methods and techniques. It would be about loving people first....And that means all people everywhere, not just your family or your own countrymen or your own color. And wanting for them what you want for yourself. And then next is respect for people's abilities to learn and to act and to shape their own lives. I think our job is try to figure out ways to help people take over their own lives.

Myles Horton

....

In our rush to reform education, we have forgotten a simple truth: reform will never be achieved by renewing appropriations, restructuring schools, rewriting curricula, revising texts if we continue to demean and dishearten the human resource called the teacher upon whom so much depends.

Parker Palmer

If learning is going to be worth much, it requires discipline and persistence on the students' part—a willingness to acknowledge that subjects are complex, that learning is hard, and that it is only by doing and re-doing that real quality is produced. On the teacher's' part, it similarly requires the creativity to craft challenges that will capture the students' imagination—often by taking what is on the surface and setting it slightly askew—and it requires the exceptionally careful planning and attention to detail that, together, organize how that learning will be carried out.

Jal Mehta

Prejudices, it is well known, are most difficult to eradicate from the heart whose soil has never been loosened or fertilized by education: they grow there, firm as weeds among stones.

Charlotte Bronte

Schools don't have to choose between high levels of mastery of knowledge and skills and students full of joy in learning who are becoming great human beings and contributing actively to the betterment of their communities.

Scott Hartl

"Accountability" is not just testing. It can also be accountability to learning and quality, to colleagues and community.

Steve Seidel

...of all the issues in education, the issue of relevance is the phoniest. If life were as predictable and small as the talkers of politics would have it, then relevance would be a consideration. But life is large and surprising and mysterious, and we don't know what we need to know. When I was a student I refused certain subjects because I thought they were irrelevant to the duties of a writer, and I have had to take them up, clumsily and late to understand my duties as a man. What we need in education is not relevance but abundance, variety, adventurousness, thoroughness. A student should suppose that he needs to learn everything he can, and he should suppose he will need to know much more than he can learn.

Wendell Berry

I became more courageous by doing the very things I needed to be courageous for—first, a little, and badly. Then, bit by bit, more and better. Being avidly—sometimes annoyingly—curious and persistent about discovering how others were doing what I wanted to do.

Audre Lorde

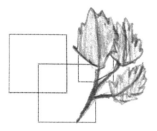

Education is not preparation for life; education is life itself.

John Dewey

What it means to be human is to bring up your children in safety, educate them, keep them healthy, teach them how to care for themselves and others, allow them to develop in their own way among adults who are sane and responsible, who know the value of the world and not its economic potential. It means art, it means time, it means all the invisibles never counted by the GDP and the census figures. It means knowing that life has an inside as well as an outside. And I think it means love.

Jeanette Winterson

There is more to life than increasing its speed.

Ghandi

Education either functions as an instrument which is used to facilitate integration of the younger generation into the logic of the present system and bring about conformity or it becomes the practice of freedom, the means by which men and women deal critically and creatively with reality and discover how to participate in the transformation of their world.

Richard Shaull

EXPEDITION REFLECTION

I felt like a real scientist looking into a microscope, and when I found the specimen I felt awesome! When we walked to other ponds as a class, it seemed weird, but fun because it was out of the ordinary. When I sat down in the grass and had written down some information about the ponds, it felt like I was a reporter. Observing the scene you have to make sure you get everything down because you want the front page. When you're done with the expedition you go home and tell your Mom and Dad what you learned. They practically don't even know what you're talking about. It's like you wrote a new chapter in the encyclopedia. Six weeks ago I would have never known about pond life.

From an EL Education student's expedition journal

For apart from inquiry, apart from the praxis, individuals cannot be truly human. Knowledge emerges only through invention and re-invention, through the restless, impatient, continuing, hopeful inquiry human beings pursue in the world, with the world, and with each other.

Paulo Freire

Tabitha Brown is six years old in the first grade. Her teacher says that she's "a dreamer." She sits there sometimes in her class in vague ambiguous delight as if her thoughts are in a sweeter land than ours...

Tabitha looks up. The teacher bends over her chair and looks into her eyes, then opens her textbook to the proper page and centers it before her on the desk. Tabitha sits up erect and tries to concentrate.

The teacher is gentle with her. It's still morning in New York, and very early morning in this child's life. Good teachers don't approach a child of this age with overzealousness or destructive conscientiousness. They're not drill-masters in the military or floor managers in a production system. They are specialists in opening small packages. They give the string a tug but do it carefully. They don't know yet what's in the box. They don't know if it's breakable.

From *Ordinary Resurrections*, by Jonathan Kozol

Education is a human right with immense power to transform. On its foundation rest the cornerstones of freedom, democracy and sustainable human development.

Kofi Annan

It is easier to build strong children than to repair broken men.

Frederick Douglass

Being a teacher at an EL school means that we are encouraged to think both broadly and deeply about what is really important. The whole process of designing an EL learning experience forces me, as a teacher, to be clear and focused and to continually evaluate why I do what I do. It means that my students see that they have options in life, can make choices, and can create their own best learning experiences.

On a purely practical level it's a lot of work, constantly looking for those ways to deepen the experience for my students. But it is the work that makes me want to get up every morning, to come back. The stimulation provided to me professionally and personally is the fuel of my passion for teaching.

Maeta Kaplan

We can't continue to treat schools as a place to train children into compliance with authoritarians. It's too dangerous. We like protest when white adults do it in marches, but we don't like protest when black kids do it in the form of righteous anger. We have to learn to see these children as powerful, as our best hope for a different, more human way.

Carla Shalaby

Teachers can only be teachers when there are students who want to be students. Without a question, an answer is experienced as manipulation; without a struggle, help is considered interference, and without the desire to learn, the offer to teach is easily felt as oppression. Therefore, our first task is not to offer information, advice, or even guidance, but to allow others to come into touch with their own struggles, pains, doubts, and insecurities—in short, to affirm their life as a quest.

Henri Nouwen

Whoever touches the life of the child touches the most sensitive point of a whole which has roots in the most distant past and climbs toward the infinite future. Whoever touches the child touches the vital and delicate point where all can be renewed, where all is pulsating with life, where the secrets of the soul lay hidden. To work consciously for the child and to go deep down, with the tremendous intention of understanding him, would be to conquer the secrets of mankind, just as so many secrets of nature have been conquered in the world around us. The activity of the child has always been looked upon as an expression of his vitality. But his activity is really the work he performs in building up the man he is to become. It is the incarnation of the human spirit.

Maria Montessori

The great aim of education is not knowledge, but action.

Herbert Spencer

We must not underestimate the urgency of a student's school life. In four years the average high school student will spend five thousand hours inside our halls. This is time kids never get back— time they cannot use to talk with their parents, learn to play the banjo, or ponder life's mysteries with a great book. It is valuable time. It is, in fact, the most important time kids will spend during their teenage years. We must use it well.

George Wood

Teaching is mostly listening and learning is mostly telling.

Deborah Meier

There can be no doubt that the youth of today have to be protected against certain poisonous effects inherent in present-day civilization. Five social diseases surround them, even in early childhood. There is the decline in fitness due to modern methods of locomotion; the decline in initiative due to the widespread disease of spectatoritis; the decline in care and skill due to the weakened tradition of craftsmanship; the decline in self-discipline due to the ever-present availability of tranquilizers and stimulants, and the decline in compassion, which William Temple called "spiritual death."

Kurt Hahn

POEMS—A SHORT LIST OF FAVORITES

As a final celebration of Hahn's words, "There is more in us than we know," and in honor of the 25th anniversary of EL Education, we offer this short list of 25 favorite poems. Go online, search by title, and enjoy.

Before You Know What Kindness Really Is
Naomi Shihab Nye

Blessing the Boats
Lucille Clifton

Did I Miss Anything?
Tom Wayman

Eagle Poem
Joy Harjo

Everything is Waiting for You
David Whyte

Fire
Judy Brown

The Fountain
Denise Levertov

Go to the Limits of Your Longing
Rainer Maria Rilke

God Says Yes to Me
Kaylin Haught

The Guest House
Rumi

Harlem
Langston Hughes

INDEX

INDEX

INDEX

INDEX

ABOUT EL EDUCATION

EL Education is a leading national K–12 nonprofit helping to build great schools in diverse communities across America.

For over 25 years, EL Education has been bringing to life an expanded vision of student achievement that includes mastery of knowledge and skills, character, and high-quality student work. EL Education promotes active classrooms: *alive* with discovery, problem-solving, challenge, and collaboration. EL Education drives *results*: teachers fulfill their highest aspirations and students achieve more than they think possible. EL Education students have both the capacity and the passion to build a better, more just world.

EL Education's expert educators work with schools (both district and charter) across 35 states, serving over 200,000 students and 16,000 teachers in our school network and multi-year literacy partnerships. Rigorous impact studies by Mathematica Policy Research demonstrate that EL Education's approach works: teachers significantly improve their craft and students achieve more, regardless of background.

Grounded in decades of in-depth work with educators, EL Education creates highly respected, widely distributed open educational resources, including the following: the world's largest collection of exemplary student projects; an acclaimed literacy curriculum that has been downloaded 8.7 million times and received the

highest possible ratings from EdReports; inspiring instructional videos with over 1.3 million views; hundreds of free online resources; and best-selling education books.

EL Education was founded in 1992 by the Harvard Graduate School of Education in collaboration with Outward Bound USA, based on the belief that learning and achievement flourish when teachers and students are engaged in work that is challenging, adventurous, and meaningful.

ELeducation.org

YOUR ADDITIONS

There Is More In Us Than We Know

YOUR ADDITIONS

YOUR ADDITIONS

There Is More In Us Than We Know

YOUR ADDITIONS

YOUR ADDITIONS

There Is More In Us Than We Know

YOUR ADDITIONS

YOUR ADDITIONS

There Is More In Us Than We Know